JOURNAL

PETER PAUPER PRESS, INC.
WHITE PLAINS, NEW YORK

Cover image by La Shae V. Ortiz

Copyright © 2008
Peter Pauper Press, Inc.
202 Mamaroneck Avenue
White Plains, NY 10601
All rights reserved
ISBN 978-1-59359-487-9
Printed in China
8

Visit us at www.peterpauper.com